SO FAITHFUL.

SO FAITHFUL.

DAVID T. GILBERT.

Order this book online at www.trafford.com
or email orders@trafford.com

Most Trafford titles are also available at major online book retailers.

Printed in the United States of America.

ISBN: 978-1-4669-1502-2 (sc)
ISBN: 978-1-4669-1501-5 (e)

Trafford rev. 04/28/2012

 www.trafford.com

North America & international
toll-free: 1 888 232 4444 (USA & Canada)
phone: 250 383 6864 ♦ fax: 812 355 4082

CONTENTS

AUTHOR'S NOTE

PLEASE TAKE NOTE that those poems contained within this book that express a point of view, or an opinion about life principles, should not be regarded as 'absolute truth', but should be interpreted as by the above, as a point of view or an opinion only.

I have been with the Lord now for the best part of 32 years, and what I have written about was due to what I have observed within a Church situation, or because of observance through the eyes of a Spirit filled, born again believer.

All of the work that I do is actually based on fact, or factual events, and is due to having preference to writing about those things that occurred in my life that are based on truth, or have been experienced by me first hand.

I believe very strongly that when the task that one puts one's hand to is based on fact and truth, then that work becomes an expression of the individuals character, and therefore comes with all the heart felt emotion that the individual has.

As for my opinion, or point of view on the work in question, these expressions are how I interpreted the situations and circumstances that I went through at that particular time, what I was thinking, and what I was going through emotionally, and spiritually. Everyone is entitled to an opinion, and all should be permitted to express that opinion in a peace-ful, non violent way, without duress.

I have chosen to express my opinion through my poetry, in order to stir up peaceful, open debate, and therefore open up opportunities for salvation, and maybe bring people into an awareness that, we serve a God who has no wish, or desire, to see anyone go to a lost eternity.

God has given us a choice, in which He will not interfere with, but regardless of our final decision, He will respect that decision, and grant your desire, so choose wisely. God bless your choosing, regardless,

David T. Gilbert.

INTRODUCTION

To INTRODUCE THIS third book, I feel it necessary to explain a little of my motivation for writing what I have in the way I have. My main focus has been on salvations, but in my thinking, to have a God given talent and not use it for His Glory would be like burying ones head in the sand dunes of missed opportunities. My main talents are encouragement and strength of character, but recently I have noticed that steadfastness, stability and faithful-ness have come to the surface. My Christian walk has been very interesting, to say the least, and has not been without it's challenges and slip ups, but after my encounter with the Lord, and the way He changed me from inside, I felt it so much easier to love than to take offence and hate. That is why I have always tried to keep my attitude in check, at all times and in every situation, since good role models are a bit of a rarity these days. And because of this, I have gained the respect of many, if not most, of my friends at my local church.

In writing my life story, I took my example to a whole new level, with the motivation of using my talents to reach people for Jesus. In my years as a servant of God, I have never been a Pastor, never had any great influence with people and basically have nothing going for me, except what I have received from the Lord. Yet I have brought some of the biggest problem people to Church, but even though they are not in Church today, they at least had a chance for salvation that they would never have otherwise had.

My poetry is written in such a way as to challenge ones thinking, and provide an opportunity to debate peacefully what is written, and hopefully open a door for people to make a decision for Christ. I am not too concerned about becoming rich or famous, and being a popular mister nice guy has little appeal to me, but when it comes to reaching people for the Lord, I would rather see others excel than myself. My God has been so faithful to me, and merciful in many ways, I just have a burning passion to serve Him with excellence and integrity, using my talents to magnify His name and populate heaven.

I trust that all the readers of this book are somehow inspired and motivated to live a life worthy of Him, and be stirred into action to be men and women of integrity for His glory,

May all be blessed and encouraged, as you read,

David T. Gilbert.

INTRODUCTION TO 'SO FAITHFUL'

IN THIS POEM, I wrote these words to express my appreciation to my God for all that He has done for me, but how does anyone truly give thanks to God for what He has done. There are times when words are not enough, and they must be supported by actions, and a good heart attitude. The reason for this poem, is that by meditating on what is written, you may also declare that Jesus is Lord, not because you read it in a book, but because you know that He is in your heart. Be blessed as you read and enjoy,

David T. Gilbert.

So Faithful

(1)   My God is so faithful,

        He's omnipotently stable,

           He is worthy of the highest praise,

    His love will ever be,

        Joyfully watching over me,

           I'm kept safe for all my days.

(2)   His grace is amazing,

        I just can't stop praising,

           He accepts us at our pace,

    His love is totally,

        Overwhelming to me,

           At the cross, He took my place.

(3)   God has no need to be,

        Displaying His glory,

           He is at ease with who He is,

    When we surrender to Him,

        He forgives us of sin,

           Then invites us to be one of His.

(4)   I could hardly believe,

        The love I'd receive,

            It touches the depths of your soul,

No one could show love,

      As Jesus surely does,

         By His stripes, I have been made whole.

(5)   He opened my eyes,

        To my great surprise,

            Then, I finally understood,

His plan for my life,

      Was to be with my wife,

         And live my life for His good.

(6)   He is so Holy,

        I think of Him only,

            Nothing else compares to Him,

We run our own race,

      By way of his Grace,

         His Spirit abides deep within.

(7)   Honour and favour,

        Are bestowed by the Saviour,

            Upon His faithful ones,

His promise to all,

      Is a life that won't fall,

         In the Kingdom of His Son.

(8)   It's so good to savour,

        Of His gracious Favour,

           To be called, 'The anointed of God',

  When you know that you're loved,

        By the Father above,

           You have boldness to declare His Word.

(9)   I love Him to the end,

        My Companion, my Friend,

           He will always be my #1,

  Very soon, I will see,

        He's Coming back for me,

           Then, I will shine like the sun.

(10)   He has saved my life,

        From trouble and strife,

           He is my Strength and Shield,

  I will serve Him faithfully,

        Each day that I see,

           To Jesus only, shall I yield.

(11)   Each morning I see,

        New mercies for me,

           I'm so thankful for peace in my heart,

  No matter what season,

        Or whatever reason,

           His Joy is my Strength from the start.

(12)   Everywhere I go,

      There are people I know,

         They seem to have lost all hope,

   Living each day,

      In their own, meaningless way,

         They seem to need a life rope.

(13)   When all is quite well,

      And life is so swell,

         They live their lives with great ease,

   But when the 'good' life,

      Starts causing them strife,

         Nothing they do in life can please.

(14)   There are so many lost,

      Who want to be Boss,

         They assume they have all the answers,

   If only they could realise,

      You can not fool God's eyes,

         They may surrender to 'The Master'.

(15)   My Saviour has been,

      So merciful to me,

         I seem to mess up every time,

   Each time that I sin,

      Causes Him pain within,

         I feel guilty of the ultimate crime.

(16)   But I am always aware,

        His Mercy is there,

           To cleanse me and set me free,

    Then I stand up to face,

        My Divinely planned race,

           Being all that He would have me to be.

(17)   If you don't know Jesus,

        Who came to appease us,

           I give this challenge to you,

    Repent of your sin,

        He will forgive you within,

           Transforming your life like brand new.

(18)   It does you no good,

        To say 'maybe I should',

           That's why Jesus went to the cross,

    He exchanged His pure life,

        For ours, full of strife,

           Our gain is Heaven's great loss.

(19)   The life God has planned,

        Coming from His wise hand,

           Is to give you a hope and a future,

    When Jesus comes for His bride,

        We will join the angels with pride,

           And together sing 'Hallelujah'.

(20)   As you rise each morn,

        With a brand new dawn,

           You will live each day without fear,

    He will be by your side,

        Within you abide,

           Your love will grow stronger each year.

(21)   And for those who have known,

        The Lord as their own,

           And for some reason, have turned away,

    Our God will advance,

        Giving you a second chance,

           Come and surrender, this could be your day.

(22)   My God will displace,

        His mercy and grace,

           His desire is that all should live,

    He knows all things,

        The pressure life brings,

           He is waiting to save and forgive.

(23)   For thirty years now,

        I have served, and how,

           My talent is 'encouragement',

    And now, I have poetry,

        To add to my ministry,

           I know they are 'Heaven sent'.

(24)　It's so humbling to serve,

　　　I feel so highly honored,

　　　　To be considered a 'Champion' for our Lord,

　　I encourage the youth,

　　　With words of truth,

　　　　I uplift by the Spirit's word.

(25)　I have no desire,

　　　To seek to aspire,

　　　　All Glory belongs to our SAVIOUR,

　　When we faithfully ask,

　　　Putting our hand to the task,

　　　　He anoints us to walk in His favour.

(26)　One day, we alone,

　　　Will appear at His throne,

　　　　To give account for our lives,

　　I long to hear my King,

　　　Say, as the Angels sing

　　　　'Well done, faithful servant, receive your prize'.

(27)　Until that day,

　　　I will serve in every way,

　　　　My Saviour and my King,

　　I will reflect His Glory,

　　　In telling my story,

　　　　Because He is my everything.

INTRODUCTION TO 'THANK YOU, LORD'

THIS IS A poem that is written as a guide to prayer topics, and for those who may need a bit of help in commencing a pattern of prayer. In any regard, God receives our words and confession as what we speak over our lives, so it pays to have a positive confession of faith, especially with what we tend to speak over other people's lives. I pray you have food for thought, as you read,

David T. Gilbert.

Thank you, Lord

Thank you, Lord, for Your amazing grace,
And for the honour of seeking Your face.

Thank you, Lord, for each new day,
And for blessing me with BessieMae.

Thank you, Lord, for my children, too,
For the challenge they present, in revealing You.

And thank you for my neighbours and friends,
And love and peace that never ends.

Thank you for your Spirit of Grace,
Who helps me to complete my race.

Thank you for Your favour, too,
And each new day, with mercies anew.

Thank you for Your patient love,
And a marriage blessed from heaven above.

Thank you for Your gift of wisdom,
And for Your rebuke, when I disobey Your instruction.

Thank you for reassuring me, when I act in fear,
And forgetting You are ever near.

But thank you, just for being You,
And for intimacy, when I'm feeling blue.

I have so much to be thankful for,
Each day, I love you more and more.

And thank you for the champion I am.
My life is safely in Your hand.

Lastly, thank you that I'm free,
To live for You eternally.

INTRODUCTION TO
'THE SOWER OF THE SEED'

When I sat down to write this poem, I found it quite a challenge to think about how I could put this Parable into poetry, as I wanted to include as much Biblical Truth as possible, without contradicting the Word of God, or bordering on heresy. So I sat down and went right through the Bible, studying all three accounts of the parable in the first three Gospels, taking notes and writing down points of interest. But even though writing this poem was a challenge, I must state that the wording and ideas that I used and portrayed, were and are not to be taken as absolute Biblical fact, but are meant to be used as a starting point for open, peaceful discussion, which I have intended to be an opportunity for possible salvation, or the chance thereof.

The thoughts I have expressed are from what I perceive to be the most logical and plainly obvious explanation of this particular parable, but you may have another way, or idea of explaining what the heart of the parable means. Everyone has a right to an opinion, provided that the opinion expressed is done so in an appropriate and peaceful way, and what is written is my opinion, or point of view(as I see and perceive it.).

I trust you may have some interesting in depth discussions, as you read, God bless you heaps,

David T. Gilbert.

The Sower Of The Seed

A 'Parable' is a story, from everyday life,

A comparison of moral truth, a warning of future strife,

Or an illustration of Truth, as written in God's Word,

It's story is simple, told in such a precise way,

As to motivate our thinking, to study and pray,

Hungering for the meaning of each word, as spoken by our Lord.

Jesus spoke many parables, as He walked this troubled earth,

He revealed His Father's Kingdom, and His Divine plan of 're-birth',

He said to Nicodemas one night, 'You must be born-again',

One parable He spoke, was very interesting indeed,

He spoke of a Sower, who was scattering his seed,

And the four types of soil that would welcome the scattered grain.

The theme of the parable, is how we receive what we hear,

And the foundation we build upon, be it by faith or by fear,

Our obligation is to study God's Word, to seek out the deepest Truth,

If we are true believers, in our Lord Jesus Christ,

To study God's Word is an honorable sacrifice,

Our attitude toward life and all people, will be adequate proof.

The first seed mentioned, is the seed 'along the path',

Their faith is very shallow, so they don't really last,

They see more value in this life, than the one hereafter,

They hear God's Word, but are void of understanding,

They see very little value, in obedience to God's commanding,

They would prefer to live with the lie, with mischievous joy and laughter.

The next to be mentioned, is the seed on 'rocky places',

These folk love attention, and warm, friendly embraces,

Their first reaction to God's Word is to embrace it with joy,

They never seem to appreciate, gracefully growing old,

They prefer to live life hot, as opposed to being cold,

'Let the good times roll on', for every girl and every boy.

But when they never seem, to get pampered, or a mention,

About being the main 'centre, of everyone's attention',

They quietly move on, and try starting all over again,

They never seem to dirty their gentle, soft hands,

By obeying the simplest, of God's commands,

They're too proud, and too important, to have to try and explain.

The third to be noted is the 'seed among the thorns',

Who expect to awaken every day, with the rise of a new dawn,

These are the 'material' people, of the above-mentioned group,

They never have enough, and are always in need,

They would go to any length, just to satisfy their greed,

Like a fox in Summer, with a defenseless chicken coup.

These are never satisfied, they always hunger for more,

They make themselves rich, by robbing the poor,

Their focus is on what they can get for absolute zip,

But there is a great Judge, up in Heaven above,

Who hates injustice, but protects those He loves,

He will deal with all justly, shooting straight from the hip.

The last to be mentioned, is the 'seed on good soil',

These are committed, to faithfully labor and toil,

Retaining God's Word in their hearts, like 'Pirates treasure',

They won't value their life, in light of His Word,

Jesus is the most precious, name to be ever heard,

Their focus is on what brings our Saviour the greatest pleasure.

These people have abandoned their carnal life,

They know that they were purchased, by Jesus' sacrifice,

God's Holy Spirit protects them, wherever they should go.

He is their wisdom, their guide and their peace,

God's love for them will never ever cease,

They enjoy the favor of God, 'cause He loves them so.

The one thing all four groups had in common, just to mention,

They all heard God's Word, but only one group paid attention,

The seed on good soil were looking forward to a better day,

So if you know in your heart, that God is calling you,

Don't ignore His plea, and miss your privileged cue,

You are highly honored by God, in so many ways.

This may be the last chance, that you will ever get,

Make the most of your time, or else you may regret,

The opportunity you allowed to slip by will strike you with fear,

Very soon, the last trumpet will make it's sound,

By then, not a Christian on earth will be found,

So call upon Jesus, while He is still available, and quite near.

David T. Gilbert.

A Poem of Praise and Worship

When you're alone and in despair,
Just speak to Jesus, with a prayer.

If your friend is feeling low,
Intercession is the way to go.

If you're having lots of trouble,
Tongues will help you to pray double.

When you feel His arms of love,
Praise your Heavenly Father above.

Worship the God of All Creation,
And thank Him for our wonderful Nation.

When you want a prayer for healing,
Raise your hands if you are willing.

A poem written by my BessieMae!

INTRODUCTION TO OBEDIENCE

I WROTE THIS poem to illustrate how challenging it can be, at times, to be as obedient as described in the Bible, and to show also that we mere mortals are not as perfect as we would like to assume we are. I trust that you will be enlightened, as you read,

David T. Gilbert.

The Struggle With OBEDIENCE

When I first surrendered to the Lord,
It was such an awesome thing,
I experienced God's love, peace, and grace,
And freedom from all my sin.

I was so thankful to the Lord,
For the sacrifice He gave,
He released me, then He raised me up,
To be His Champion, so brave.

The Spirit Dwells inside of me,
I now am born-again,
I am so honored to be a part,
Of His heavenly domain.

I have served my Lord many years,
As an example of His love,
My desire is to encourage all folk I meet,
Reflecting His Glory above.

I love to study God's Holy Word,
Like unearthing Pirate's treasure,
There are so many fascinating stories,
Bible reading is my pleasure.

I introduced Jesus to my friends,
By giving my testimony,
I wrote a book about my life,
Bought by those who know me.

My reputation amongst the flock,
Was awesome, to say the least,
I was a legend, and a champion,
On God's blessing, I would feast.

Then one day, whilst studying God's Word,
I came across mighty Saul,
He was anointed to be a King,
Until his tragic fall.

He was given a specific task to do,
With very precise instructions,
But instead of doing as Samuel said,
He followed his assumptions.

He was told to kill every human found,
Within the Amalekite clan,
But he killed the worst, and spared the best,
He was proved a foolish man.

God wasn't pleased with Saul at all,
It was such a tragic day,
To sacrifice means zip to God,
If you're not willing to OBEY.

Acting upon what you assume,
Is foolishness to our Lord,
He requires our obedience,
To carry out His Word.

At times, we see our talents within,
And how useful they can be,
But to move without the presence of God,
Is living very dangerously.

No matter what area of Ministry, or task,
Regardless of who you are,
To sacrifice for God is good,
But to obey is better by far.

God knows everything that happens,
He is never caught by surprise,
He knew you before He created Earth,
Who is true, and who tells lies.

He knows of every second you live,
He knows just what you think,
Who you'll marry, your children's names,
What drives you to the brink.

When God created Adam and Eve,
He gave Adam a task to do,
To exercise God's authority and power,
And have dominion too.

But when Adam dropped the baton,
God put His plan in place,
He sent His only begotten Son,
To die for the human race.

Jesus was obedient unto death,
He paid sin's price for us all,
But some of us are so keen to please,
We try to walk before we can crawl.

I know my Lord as a timely Friend,
He is always by my side,
His Angels ever watch over me,
His Spirit in me abides.

I love my Jesus far too much,
To want to disobey,
I don't always get it right,
But I do my best each day.

At times, God tells us to relax,
Take time out for refreshing,
We need to revive and recuperate,
In order to flow in the blessing.

When we serve Him in obedience,
Without the question, 'Why',
All things turn out according to plan,
Good news for you and I.

The greatest victories in our lives,
Are achieved through obedience,
Even when it seems so futile,
And nothing ever makes sense.

God knows what is happening,
He sees the things we don't,
He wants us all to trust in Him,
But there are so many who won't.

I know my Lord is with me,
He greets me each new morn,
I talk with Jesus every day,
Even when mowing the lawn.

So, if you truly love the Lord,
Obedience won't be any issue,
Even if all He did was save,
His praise would still be due.

He really owes us nothing at all,
We serve Him, 'cause of His Grace,
To truly be obedient to Him,
Is to trust Him in every place.

If we saw God, as He truly is,
In all His Majesty and Glory,
We'd be too terrified to disobey,
Our walk would be so Holy.

Our God is more than able,

To do more that we perceive,

But in order to be obedient,

We must first truly believe.

David T. Gilbert.

INTRODUCTION TO 'NEVER SAY DIE'

THIS IS A poem that means a lot to me, since my main area of influence in my Church is the Youth, I just love speaking into their lives, as they receive encouragement very enthusiastically. I have a healthy respect for the Youth, and try my best to lift their spirits whenever I am able to, be-cause the peer pressure my generation faced was nothing to what our Youth face today. With technology ever advancing, and money, as we have known it in the past, being modified each year to cater for our ever advancing economical society, is it any wonder that our confused and mixed up young ones would rather face death, than live any longer in a world spinning out of control!

My aim in this poem is to bring back a little hope to those youth who, for obvious reasons, have lost sight of the hope that our God promises, or are a bit fed up with the battle, and are in need of someone who cares enough to want to see them win their race, crossing the finish line as only a champion could do. But most of all, see them run their race in a way that would give them a 'Never Say Die' attitude, and finally receiving the victor's crown.

I pray that you, especially if you are Youth, find a renewed strength and a determination to win, at all cost, as you read,

God bless you in abundance,
David T. Gilbert.

Never Say Die

To all who are Youth, both young and old,
This poem is for you, to help you to be bold.

When you gave your heart, yielding all to Christ,
You started a journey, that would consume your life.

When God chose you, He revealed His plan,
A race marked for all, both woman and man.

It's the same race described, in God's Holy Word,
Where Paul says, 'make every step, count for the Lord.

Our salvation is our start, His joy is our strength,
The Spirit is our Tutor, as we serve God at length.

Perseverance and Endurance, are keys to your race,
While Focus and Determination, will help you keep pace.

Many obstacles will be faced, disguised in strange ways,
Some are even odd things, that upset your days.

There are those who will question, or shake your Faith,
But no man is worthy, we are saved by Grace.

Your new life and thinking, what you morally believe,
May be scrutinised by friends, what you have, they envy.

This world has lost control, there's no hope at all,
You could be their life rope, to stop their sad fall.

Every temptation we face, is a fork in our road,
We have the right to choose, if we want sin's heavy load.

Born losers are not part, of God's plan to win,
We believe God is Holy, our destiny lies within.

The confession we speak, we should never take lightly,
Life and death are in our power, it's wisdom to speak rightly.

I was raised up to be, a Champion for God's cause,
To encourage those of God, so they may run their course.

I was also to be an example, of a proper attitude,
To those who look on, showing God their gratitude.

In my past, I would swear, showing hatred to all,
But now, I want to love, saving people from their fall.

The words that I speak, are to give you hope and trust,
To help you run to win, and leave the world for dust.

So, I encourage you all, to run as if to win,
Never give up, never yield, and never give in.

No matter how many times, you get it all wrong,
Get up and keep running, determine to finish strong.

Don't worry about tomorrow, or listen to negative talk,
Don't consider embracing evil, or changing your walk.

Keep focused on the Lord, looking neither left or right,
Your Crown is to His Glory, you are precious in His sight.

Don't ever receive the false, and never accept a lie,
Tune your ears to the Truth, you're the apple of His eye.

So now you have a word, to give you strength and hope,
When the going gets tough, use this poem as a life rope.

Remember, our precious God, will love us to the end,
My encouragement is to you, God bless you, my dear friend.

David T. Gilbert.

INTRODUCTION TO 'CONSISTENCY'

THIS IS A poem that has been on my heart for some time, as it contains a subject along the lines of what I love to write about. My focus in writ-ing is to present to people the things that have been put aside, when it comes to living life according to basic Christian principles and morality.

There are times in our walk with Christ, that we get so caught up with filling our heads with knowledge, that we tend to forget how to simply and humbly walk with God as we are, instead of how we interpret the way we assume God wants us to walk. Being consistent in all you do not only shows people that you are the genuine article, it has a drawing effect on people which opens doors of opportunity to lead them to salvation. It also pleases your Father above as you walk, according to His will, not our own. I pray that you be blessed as you read,

David T. Gilbert.

Consistency

Consistency is one of those quiet words,
Often referred to, but rarely ever heard.

Most people I know, omit from their life,
This word that would assist them, and help them through strife.

To be consistent should not be, thought of as so cheap,
Your Father in Heaven, is observing as you sleep.

He values consistency, in all that we do,
In attitude, in conduct, and example, too.

Consistency means that, your thoughts and your actions,
Line up with His will, to God's satisfaction.

It means you are working, as one does with another,
But not necessarily, with your Sister or Brother.

Consistency brings harmony, if it's outworked God's way,
Meaning your thinking is the same, as it was yesterday.

You don't have mood swings, and you don't change your mind,
Peace replaces confusion, for some, just in time.

People know you by reputation, you are always the same,
You're a pleasure to meet, and they call you by name.

I have found many times, people avoid anger and strife,
They shun inconsistency, and run for their life.

As you live a life far, from disruptive confusion,
Loving all consistently, they welcome your intrusion.

I love friendly people, I call everyone a 'Champ',
I am greeted with honor, I have their approval stamp.

I try my very best, to show consistency to all,
I have no favorites, cause I love great and small.

I consider all a friend, cause I love as Jesus would,
I would spend all day with Him, if only I could.

My gift is encouragement, it consumes me like a flame,
I am so passionate about telling all, Jesus loves you the same.

God gave me a 'Barnabas' spirit, to be a great strength,
To all that I talk to, and encourage, at length.

But if I was inconsistent, and thought it a joke,
I would have not a friend, I would be a pitiful bloke.

But I can praise God, I am good at what I do,
It's with His enabling, that I encourage all of you.

People say I am awesome, I make them feel good,
I am so highly honored, to encourage as Jesus would.

I have no real desire, to seek my own glory,
I am an ACE for Jesus, but that's another story.

So, if you want to be a winner, not just one of the crowd,
Show consistency in all you do, and your Saviour will be proud.

You will stand as a rock, like you would amongst giants,
Facing your adversary, in stubborn defiance.

Your faith in your God, will be an unshakeable one,
Then when Jesus returns, you will shine like the SON.

David T. Gilbert.

INTRODUCTION TO
'THE SIGNIFICANCE OF TITHING'

THIS POEM IS about tithing, it's significance to God and us, and the importance of tithing when it comes to honouring God. The giving of tithes on Sundays as a regular part of our worship, is both controversial and sensitive, to say the least, but when it is seen in the light of 1 Corinthians 9: 13 & 14, then tithing becomes more of a God issue than a material issue. Tithing is, firstly, honouring God with the first part of what we rely on most, our wage, thus providing us with a means to daily live. Our dependence is on God for our survival, and we are giving thanks to Him for our provision, since the ability to create wealth is by His grace (Psalm 112: 3; Proverbs 3: 9 & 10). Secondly, tithing provides your Pastors with their wage, so just imagine if your boss expected you to work for him underpaid, or not paid at all, the better your Pastors look is a reflection on how well you honour the tithe. My aim is to stir your thinking about tithing, and see it in a new light, so, be enlightened as you read,

David T. Gilbert.

The Significance of Tithing

As written in God's Holy Word,
The tithe is sacred to the Lord,
We pay our tithes in honour of our King.
It's God who blesses us with wealth,
Providing us with daily health,
He knows our hearts, and He knows everything.

He sees our attitude as we give,
For some, it helps us just to live,
But for most, we give from a humble, open heart,
Some give in worship to our Saviour,
Others give to win His favour,
In regards to worship, tithing plays a significant part.

Tithing is worshipping the Lord of Hosts,
Thanking Him for the Holy Ghost,
Yet tithing comes in many different ways,
There is gambling, alcohol, and sexual sin,
Robbing you of God's peace within,
Living for self will surely shorten your days.

We complain that the Church is after our money,

Now, don't you think that's rather funny,

We dare not live without our beer and smokes,

Or ten bucks on the daily double,

Just to save us from our trouble,

In the end, you are seen as just 'one of the blokes'.

Tithing is honour to our King,

Living for Him is everything,

The tithe is fitting for a Righteous God,

Tithing is by faith in Him,

Unless we tithe, life seems so dim,

It's believing in His Holy written Word.

Tithing is showing your dependence on heaven,

Especially in 2 Corinthians 9: 6 & 7,

God loves a cheerful giver, from the heart,

Our attitude in the way we give,

Will encourage others on how to live,

And be an example to them on how to start.

Tithing is a principle, not a law,

The more you give, you'll get for sure,

Patience is an essential way to go,

Things won't happen overnight,

There are times you need to hold on tight,

Persistence is the key to continued growth.

God honours those who honour the tithe,
He sustains them daily, and keeps them alive,
His children are the apple of His eye,
His favour rests with those He loves,
Who do what is right, as in heaven above,
Very soon, we will meet Him in the sky.

INTRODUCTION TO 'WHAT MORE CAN BE SAID'?

I WROTE THIS poem to bring people's attention to the fact that everything that can be said about the Lord of Glory has already been said in the Word of God. The words of the Bible glorify the Son of God in every way, and all we could ever hope to do is express our own personal gratitude to God from our hearts. Indeed, the Bible is a guide to not only how we should live, but also to how we should worship and glorify our Saviour, the Psalms are great for wanting to worship our God, as they are expressions of gratitude and praise from the heart. I trust that you will find a deeper faith in Christ, and a richer worship time as you read,

David T. Gilbert.

What more can be said?

What more can be said, to exalt the Lord of Glory,
What more is there to say, to complete salvations story,

No word can be uttered, just to describe it better,
No song can be sung, to enhance the written letter,

The Bible says it all, to glorify the Son,
All glory goes to Him, to heaven's Holy One.

He finished His work at Calvary, when He died upon that cross,
He rose again in victor, to show who is the Boss.

He cleansed me with His precious blood, and made me white as snow,
Filling me with His Holy Spirit, I'm His, from head to toe.

The Bible is the Word of God, the Christian's Holy book,
Containing words of Wisdom and Faith, and Hope that's worth a look.

Life presents many challenges, the trials we face are many,
The answers are in God's Holy book, and won't cost you a penny.

So open up the Word of God, and diligently study on,
Soon you'll walk in victory, your joy will make you strong.

No weapon formed against you, will ever really stand,
Our adversary can only rant and rave, you're safe in God's right hand.

So stand up all you Champions, be of courage and good cheer,
We walk by faith in the Son of God, in Him there is no fear.

Written and Edited, 9/12/2011, by David T. Gilbert.

Word count = 374, A4 pages = 2.

INTRODUCTION TO 'A LIFE WITHOUT GOD'

THIS IS A poem I wrote in light of Ephesians 4: 17-19, which describes the tragic consequences associated with a life free from God, and how we should live as Children of Light. As always, the choice is ours to yield to God in obedience, or have a life as described above, which is really not much of a life at all.

I trust that this topic will help people to open up, and express their point of view,

David T. Gilbert.

A Life Without God

In the presence of our Saviour God,
Is love, peace, joy and praise,
Wisdom and understanding abide,
In the hands of the Ancient of Days.

God created us with an eternal plan,
To be totally devoted to Him,
Intimacy and obedience are paramount,
For a life transformed from within.

But in the book of Ephesians, chapter four,
We are taught how to live as we should,
God has called us to a Holy life,
Showing love to all, for His good.

The Holy life we are called to live,
Is different from the carnal world,
In contrast to the sinners life,
Our life with Christ is jewelled.

As a sinner, your thinking becomes futile,
Your fantasies take you way off track,
Your vision is darkened from God's pure Truth,
In your focus, you start looking back.

Soon, you are separated from your walk with God,
By your lack of knowledge regarding sin,
You make excuses to justify your wrong,
Your life becomes a lie within.

You then stop reading God's Holy Word,
So subtle is the deceptive lie,
Your ignorance is obvious, your defence falls flat,
Your chance for salvation drifts by.

Your heart turns cold, and quite insensitive,
Compassion is the last thing on your mind,
Your spirit becomes opinionated and unteachable,
Ignoring the wisest advice, as you'll find.

Pleasing the flesh is your daily obligation,
It's the way that you desire to live,
Craving for pleasure, by an uncontrollable habit,
You become unbearably annoying to live with.

Following this path will lead you to hell,
Your tragic life is one to forget,
You hardly noticed when your fate was sealed,
Looking back, you have only regret.

Your life doesn't need to end this way,
It holds more value than you think,
To God, we are all valued and loved in His sight,
You need not live your life on the brink.

The Bible is God's instruction manual,
Preparing us for an eternal home,
We will be dwelling with the 'King of All Kings',
Never again to blindly roam.

So if you want to live in peace,
With the God of all Creation,
Surrender to Him, when He calls,
And change your sad situation.

David T. Gilbert.

INTRODUCTION TO 'HOW FOOLISH'

HERE IS A poem for those who think that living a double life before God can be done without a single soul knowing any different, and that not even God has eyes to see. But we all know that in the end, we can not make God look the fool, as Galatians 6:7 states, that we are to be Holy, as He is Holy, & we are to work at our salvation with fear and trembling,

(Phillippians 2: 12.). Also, we need to understand that, being tempted is not a sin, but by entertaining even the slightest thought, we open a door for us to be in a position that causes us to eventually yield to the tempt-ation we are faced with.

Finally, we need to also see that it isn't a sign of weakness or shame to cry out for help, it's just your humanity showing through, but if left undealt with, you will finish up in shame.

Be enlightened as you read,

David T. Gilbert.

How Foolish

Have you ever heard, or maybe you've known,
People who seem to live, a different life at home,
Than they do, any Sunday, in a world of their own,
How foolish, do you think we are?

We see them on Sundays, so Holy and pure,
Helping any soul, to faithfully endure,
But home life is confused, in need of a cure,
How Pretensive, do you think we are?

'Who should I pretend to be today?',
I overheard a family man say,
For some, it's just a game they play,
How Childish, do you think we are?

Should I appear as the cool, suave gent?,
Maybe the Husband from Heaven sent?,
Or even the Home Group President?,
How Perfect, do you think we are?

Pretending your Family is the perfect one,
Life seems a party, you're all having fun,
Ignoring the warnings of God's only Son,
How Deaf, do you think we are?

Your marriage, it seems, is a perfect example,

Love for each other, there is more than ample,

But your children are victims, of a love triangle,

How Immoral, do you think we are?

Having love, for those not your own,

Looking important, on your mobile phone,

While your Family is facing life alone,

How High-minded, do you think we are?

Involved in a Ministry, you know little about,

You seem very important, having plenty of clout,

At home, there is nothing but fear and doubt,

How Blind, do you think we are?

You cry out to God, just to save your skin,

Knowing that trouble lies deep within,

Still trying to hide, that secret sin,

How Deceptive, do you think we are?

At home, your life is crashing down,

The neighbourhood knows, the word spreads around,

While at Church, you stand on 'Hallowed' ground,

How Corrupt, do you think we are?

Your Family yell and scream at each other,

Those nosey neighbours, you send running for cover,

But at Church, you truly love your Brother,

How False, do you think we are?

At Church, you are the coolest of all,
Your counsel seems wise, you stand up tall,
While at home, it's like a free-for-all,
How Hollow, do you think we are?

At the Superstore, the kids give you trouble,
You throw $20.00, on the 'Daily-Double',
Your Family is in ruins, like a pile of rubble,
How Double-minded, do you think we are?

At work, you're just 'one of the blokes',
Having a laugh, while enjoying a smoke,
While your Family becomes, the neighbourhood joke,
How Rebellious, do you think we are?

Eventually, the cracks begin to show,
You can't hide any more, all your friends know,
Your life is a lie, quite an embarrassing blow,
How Disgraceful, do you think we are?

What games we play, to hide our sin,
We try to bluff God, but He knows what's within,
We must be true, and accountable to Him,
How Merciful, do you think we are?

You can't fool God, when it comes to Salvation,
No matter what colour, regardless of Nation,
It's ours to determine, our final destination,
How Choosy, do you think we are?

Be truthful, and totally honest with yourself,
Don't hang your problems on the shelf,
Ask for assistance, for your Family's health,
How Forgiving, do you think we are?

The Angels are taking note of all,
Every idle word spoken, and acts to recall,
By your own confession, you will rise or fall,
How Accountable, do you think we are?

I surrendered to Christ, without regret,
I would rather be honest, it causes less fret,
Still there are those, who haven't learned yet,
How Wrong, do you think we are?

We all need to carry, and share the blame,
Jesus willingly died, for our sin and shame,
Three days later, He had risen again,
How Loving, do you think we are?

No matter how bad your life has been,
Or even how your attitude is seen,
Come as you are, He'll make you clean,
How Caring, do you think we are?

The Spirit of God is calling, 'please',
While there's still time, get on your knees,
He offers you life, abundantly,
How Blessed, do you think we are?

I've lived my life, with many a blow,

I was rebellious once, not nice to know,

Now that I am saved, to Heaven, I'll go,

How Redeeming, do you think we are?

I give you a choice, please don't be late,

Heaven is about to close it's gates,

Don't think this a joke, or you'll find, mate,

HOW FOOLISH DO YOU THINK WE ARE?

David T. Gilbert.

INTRODUCTION TO 'BROTHERLY LOVE'

THERE ARE THOSE who are willing to stand up and protest that there is just not enough love in this world, and that we should show and greet one another in an attitude of love. But do we really mean what we say, do we really believe that Brotherly Love is possible, especially in the light of us living in a very hostile and unstable world? Dr. Martin Luther King, Jr., was a man who not only lived what he believed, but was also willing to die for it as well. I remember seeing him on the old black and white idiot box, as we used to call it, and I admired him as a man of integrity and conviction, and was very inspired by his character. In Matthew 24:12, Jesus tells us that due to the increase in wickedness, the love of most will grow cold, the evidence of that is more prevalent today than at any other time in our past history. But there is hope for the future, maybe not quite the way the world would have it, but living in perfect, pure love with the God of All Creation, sounds better to me than the alternative.

I pray you will enjoy as you read, Bless you, my Brother,

David T. Gilbert.

'Brotherly Love'

I recall when I was just a lad, a man said 'I have a dream',
He looked as if he meant it, on that black and white T. V. screen.

He spoke of peace, and brotherly love, and the content of a man's heart,
Everyone respected him highly, even though they seemed worlds apart.

It was just before J.F.K. was shot, that he walked this troubled earth,
He believed in the Almighty God above, and His plan of the new re-birth.

He stood up strong for what he believed, he was never fearful of death,
He never wavered in his faith, holding fast, till the last breath.

He was hailed as a hero of the faith, a man of conviction, for sure,
He had a solution for our troubled world, but nobody wanted to hear.

He certainly had his supporters, he was a man of integrity,
Unique in all he said and did, a true example for you and me.

His followers suffered violence and injustice, from a very unstable nation,
While the young were crying out for peace, they were called an unworthy generation.

Dr. Martin Luther King Junior, was a man ahead of his time,
Adored by many, despised by most, his death was the ultimate crime.

It isn't that easy to make a stand, when people can't see your point,
They threaten you with a violent end, or a few limbs out of joint.

When one is blinded by a one-eyed view, and can't see clearly at all,
Just ask God to broaden your scope, He'll save you from a fall.

It's such a tragic shame these days, that the world is so full of hate,
If only we could accept and love each other, before it gets too late.

I wonder, if Adam had really known, the price that mankind would pay,
By his single, absent-minded act, would he have wished to start again?

From the time of Adam, right up till now, we have all been declaring war,
We are so blinded by ourselves, we may never find the floor.

How many times have we said to our neighbour, if you need me, I'll lend a hand,
But when the need to help comes by, we just bury our heads in the sand.

If only we could speak the truth, and say just what we mean,
Instead of trying to fool ourselves, that we are squeaky clean.

Nobody lives a perfect life, we all were sinners at birth,
It's only by God's eternal Grace, we escape this crumbling earth.

You may not like God's plan at all, because you are full of hate,
But Jesus commands us to forgive, before He closes Heaven's gate.

Nobody wants to burn in hell, it wasn't meant for man,
God wants us to trust in His pure love, He's holding out His hand.

When we get to our final day, what a tragedy it would be,
To find you've followed a dead end street, missing out on eternity.

A life without God is so painfully cold, it grips your heart with fear,
But I praise Him for Amazing Grace, I know God's always near.

If you don't know the Lord of Truth, you have never felt His love,
Surrender your life, and take His hand, you will live in heaven above.

David T. Gilbert.

INTRODUCTION TO 'OLDER BROTHER BLUES'

THIS IS A poem that I wrote for a young Nephew of mine, who just couldn't get the idea as to why being the older Brother carried such an awesome responsibility, so I had to explain why, in poetry.

Older Brother Blues

I recall the life that I lived in times past,
And still do, to this present day,
I carried such a responsibility,
In an accountable and awesome way.

Being the first child to be born to my folk,
The oldest of five healthy children,
I wasn't told that I would set the example,
As the principle goes in Heaven.

The responsibility I had to see all was well,
Fell squarely at my aching feet,
My Brothers would always do as I did,
Like a herd of bewildered sheep.

They needed a role model to follow each day,
And I was the chosen one,
There were times when life just seemed too drab,
When you're the oldest of the Sons.

I was raised to be an example for good,
My influence was obvious, in time,
I could choose to lead them in honesty and truth,
Or lead them to a life of crime.

The opportunities that I missed, in leading them well,
As an accountable Brother would do,
At the time, mattered very little to me,
Because I felt like just one of the crew.

The mistakes that I made, due to misunderstanding,
Seemed too much of a burden for me,
It was quite hard going, trying to steer them right,
I felt like I had to break free.

Being the oldest Son means you're a guiding light,
A shelter from the oncoming storm,
You set the example that others will follow,
How you act will be the norm.

You may get the blame for things done wrong,
When you really were innocent of all,
But how you react to trouble like this,
Will mean that they rise or fall.

If you react in violence, so will your Brothers,
It's much better to impart God's peace,
Wisdom will keep you safe from life's storms,
Forgiveness will grant you release.

So how you act, and with all that you do,
Your Brothers are always looking on,
It's you, that needs to be well behaved,
So teach them right from wrong.

When they need someone to show them the way,
Fearing their Parents wouldn't understand,
Especially when it comes to issues of love,
They can relate to your level and plan.

If you neglect your responsibility and call,
Caring nothing for their risky plight,
Others may teach them in place of you,
And raise them in ways not quite right.

So you see, you are important to your kin,
Mistakes will always be made,
Just keep getting up and run for your life,
Your attitude will make the grade.

David T. Gilbert.

INTRODUCTION TO
'TO MY BROTHER AND FRIEND'

THIS POEM WAS written for a friend of mine, who was having a hard time at work with some of the other workers. So, I wrote this poem to try and encourage him not to give up, and not to take what they say as a person-al attack. So, read and be encouraged,

David T. Gilbert.

To my Brother and Friend

This message to my Brother and friend,
It comes from Heaven above,
From Jesus, God's one and only Son,
Who created you with His Love.

He called you for a time as this,
With a purpose and a plan,
He fashioned you and raised you up,
Your life is in His hand.

You know the Father loves you so,
Jesus showed that at Calvary,
He paid for the sin of all mankind,
By His blood, we are set free.

He died to break the power of sin,
Overcoming it's deceit and shame,
And washed you in His own shed blood,
So you may live by His Holy Name.

At work, all the others torment you,
And give you such a hard time,
It's not that God has abandoned you,
Or because you have done any crime.

The explanation is simple, but true,

And so easy to understand,

Looking through the eyes of the Spirit,

You will see His purpose and plan.

You see, God created all that is seen,

The Gospel of John tells us so,

Every person has a chance to be in God's plan,

It's their choice to say Yes or No.

At the end of the book of Revelation,

A scripture is addressed to us all,

One that gives all a choice of their own,

To accept Salvation, or fall.

The verse is in Revelation, Chapter 22,

And appears in verse 17,

It's invitation is to 'whosoever will',

It's our choice, as can plainly be seen.

We all have a choice, a personal one,

To accept Jesus as our King,

If we do, we become a child of God,

If not, we lose everything.

We serve a God of Compassion,

Who wants to give all a 'fair go',

So all have a fair chance of Salvation,

Their choice to say 'Yes' or 'No'.

You became an Ambassador for the Lord,
When you gave your life unto Him,
To represent His Kingdom authority on earth,
And turn from a life filled with sin.

The devil is our adversary,
The enemy of God above,
His kingdom is filled with hatred and strife,
God's Kingdom overflows with Love.

The devil became so angry and mean,
When you gave your life to God,
His aim is to steal, kill and destroy,
But we overcome by God's Word

At your workplace, the Spirit is watching,
Taking note of the things that are done,
Every idle word spoken, every act of rebellion,
We all stand before God's Throne.

Not a word shall be spoken, except for an eerie look,
As we peer into the eyes of Almighty God,
It will take just a glimpse, then we will know,
If we are His chosen child, or not.

Since the eyes of God can not behold sin,
But only what is pure and true,
Your life will reveal all you have done,
There is nothing you will be able to do.

Missed opportunities, the things you regret,

Trying to hide past mistakes,

All the shameful things that you will recall,

There is no one to take your place.

The chances one has, to say 'Yes to our God,

To escape their life of shame,

Were all passed up, saying 'No', without fear,

Rejecting Jesus' Holy Name.

There is no one left to save you now,

Your words will be adequate proof,

You said 'No thanks' to our God above,

Rejecting the God of Truth.

Instead, you chose to believe the lie,

And lived a life of pleasure,

You were comfortable in your blatant pride,

Satisfied to indulge in your treasure.

But here you are before Almighty God,

It's time to give account,

It's far too late to correct the past,

Before all creation, there's no doubt.

By your words, you will be declared by God,

To be innocent, or guilty of shame,

There's only one escape from an eternity in hell,

That is found 'In Jesus Name'.

You may have been their one true chance,

For them to say 'Yes' to our God,

So pray that God will open their eyes,

To the saving Grace of His Word.

Whatever they do to you, my friend,

They did all that to Jesus, too,

But, instead of getting angry, He simply said,

'Forgive them, for they know not what they do'.

He bore the shame and disgrace of sin,

Carrying all to that wooden cross,

Dying to sin, paying with His blood,

Our gain is Heaven's great loss.

So, don't be disheartened, be encouraged instead,

You have showed great boldness and faith,

Your Heavenly Father is proud of you,

You suffered for His Names sake.

It says in the Bible, when you suffer for the Lord,

We should praise His Holy Name,

You name is written in His 'Book of Life',

In Jesus, we overcame.

So praise Him, your God is well pleased,

You boldly held on by your faith,

When it is time for you to stand before God,

It will be without fear or shame'

Your reward awaits, in His Kingdom above,
Be patient, and see what's for you,
He loves you more than you could ever know'
You can trust in His Word, He is True.

INTRODUCTION TO 'THREE DIAMONDS . . . .'

THE POEM YOU are about to read is one of appreciation for three women, one Mother and two Daughters, who have been a significant encouragement and strength to me over a number of years. These women are well known to me, and are still regard-ed as Family, something that is lacking in many of our Church-es these days. These three women have left quite a significant mark on my life, and to show my love and respect for them, I have written this poem to honor them. Please enjoy reading,

David T. Gilbert.

Three Diamonds . . .

There are times in my day, I've needed someone,
To encourage and restore me, like the morning sun.

Someone who cares, when I've had a bad week,
Who knows what to say, when it's hard to speak.

Someone who is faithful, consistent and true,
Who notices problems, and helps with them too.

I have many friends, who, over many years,
Have proven their loyalty, with loving tears.

Who are more than willing, to go the extra mile,
Thinking of my good, and what makes me smile.

I need friends who love me, and care to say,
Just stop and think first, you are headed the wrong way.

Friends never take advantage, in any situation,
They focus on your benefit, never causing frustration.

When I do something stupid, like acting a fool,
My friends understand me, they've been there too.

When the pressures of life, start coming on strong,
Their smiles are enough, to last all week long.

If I am sadly lacking, in power and might,
I remain their champion, respected in their sight.

The women I refer to, are special to me,
Three Godly ladies, from the same family.

I have known these three women, for many long years,
To them, I am 'Family', they greet me with cheers.

They always show, great honour to me,
To them, I am of the highest Integrity.

Helen:

The first precious lady, is Helen, the Mum,
She is a woman of worth, her Peter's #1.

I uphold her highly, as a Sister and Friend,
A timely word keeps me, focused to the end.

Often, Helen speaks with wisdom too,
A woman of many talents, not just a few.

There are times, I have needed, some timely advice,
As only a woman could give, so purely precise.

Helen has always, put my mind straight,
Her advice is never, a moment too late.

I honor my Sister, regarding her a friend,
I will love and respect her, right to the end.

Jessica:

Jessica is good, at all she does,
She is consistent in character, greeting me with love.

I've seen Jess grow from a child, so small,
Now she is a precious, 'Woman' overall.

Jess always has a lovely heart,
Her smile gives each day an even start.

Most Sundays, Jessica comes, to worship and pray,
God smiles, as His favour guides her way.

I pray that, should she decide to marry,
He is a man most worthy, and makes her happy.

Melissa:

Last of all is Mel, as she is known to me,
Mel is a lamb, the shyest of the three.

Mel is a woman, with a lovely smile,
She's friendly, pleasant, just a little shy,

Mel always greets me as a 'Woman of Worth'
She will always be special in all the earth.

With Mel, as with Jess, I'm proud of them both,
I pray as they serve the Lord of Hosts.

These three Diamonds, are highly valued to me,
Just to know them, I am as honored as can be.

I trust that this poem, will motivate you to action,
We all could do with some 'Real' satisfaction.

Just think of somebody, who has impacted your life,
One you highly regard, not necessarily your wife.

A friend who will prove, faithful to the end,
Say, 'I am honored indeed, to know you, my friend'

A person who has influenced you, in a way that is good,
Who prays for and encourages, as a loving Brother should.

Go up and bless them, show them your love,
They may be surprised, and thank God above.

Displays of appreciation, we need to see more,
To encourage and esteem each one, as never before.

If someone offends you, go buy something nice,
It's a great way to go, in breaking the ice.

David T. Gilbert.

My Friend Joshua

My friend Joshua Marsden, is no ordinary man,
An example of Integrity, the finest in the land.

He always expresses overwhelming joy, each time that we meet,
To me, he is a Champion, from his head down to his feet.

He always reflects the Glory of God, in such a humble way,
He serves his God with faithfulness, expressing His love each day.

He always seems so keen to help, whenever there is a need,
He is such an awesome blessing, in word, in heart, indeed.

I am so proud of this young man, he is all I knew he would be,
He is a jewel in our God's crown, he will live eternally.

His smile is such a joy to behold, it reflects the love of God,
His attitude and example are, so pure and second to none.

I pray that God would bless him, in every bountiful way,
Just to know him as a friend, I am highly honoured each day.

David T. Gilbert.

INTRODUCTION TO RAY AND RITA

THIS POEM WAS written for a mature couple that I have immense honour and respect for, but because they are such humble folk, I changed the name of the two people described in this poem to protect their identity.

I wonder if you could possibly think of two people, just like Ray and Rita, that you have a high opinion of, and appreciate greatly, as I do these!

David T. Gilbert.

Ray and Rita

Ray and Rita are two precious Jewels,
In the crown of my Saviour above,
Like stars, they reflect the heart of Christ,
They are anointed by His Love.

I have known them over many years,
They are good friends of mine,
Their influence has been awesome,
And has surely been divine.

They both are very faithful,
In everything they do,
They are pillars in the Temple,
Standing steadfast, and true.

They never make a lot of noise,
They're not that type of couple,
Just quietly getting on with the job,
May God bless them double.

Ray is such a humble man,
He has a heart of gold,
The finest example to be seen,
Of Integrity, and Faith so bold.

I see him as a "Brother",
An example second to none,
In all he does, he shines forth,
The Glory of the Son.

Rita has a servant's heart,
She's so faithful, and so true,
She keeps the hosts and stewards in line,
They respect and honour her, too.

She tries so very hard to please,
Her job is quite a test,
She always makes things turn out well,
To me, she is the best.

My desire is to bless this couple,
For the friends they are to me,
They have been the type of folk,
I one day hope to be.

God bless you, Ray and Rita,
For all that you have done,
For helping me to shine for God,
Reflecting His only Son.

David T. Gilbert.

INTRODUCTION TO 'WHO IS GOOD ENOUGH FOR CHURCH, ANYWAY?'

THIS POEM EXPRESSES my thoughts and views at certain times and ages of my life, my purpose being, to help people to realize that you don't get good enough before you come to God, you come to God just as you are, and He makes you good enough!

For those who do no know God as I do, I pray that this poem may help you to answer some of those nagging little questions you may have about Christianity, and for the rest, to recall how you first encountered Christ, and reap a harvest accordingly,

God Bless you all,
David T. Gilbert.

Who Is Good Enough
For Church, Anyway?

I first became aware of God, at 5 or 6 years old,
I would go to Church with Nanna, even if it was rainy and cold,

I remember going to kindy, and learning how to pray,
I learned how Jesus loves us all, every night and every day,

But as I grew up, attending School, my interest in God would fade,
I saw myself as not worthy enough, to even make the grade,

There was no one to teach me right, I was wayward as can be,
Until an encounter with the Lord, opened my eyes to see,

By the time I reached 12 years old, I was taught about life and death,
Life sounded fine, but as for the other, it took away my breath,

I didn't know what happened to folk, after they finally died,
I couldn't see beyond the grave, with fear I often cried.

I had no knowledge to live by faith, I lived so carnally,
I sidestepped questions about the Lord, although they puzzled me.

Until one day, about midnight, I woke up full of fears,
I dreamed of death, prayed to God, my face was soaked in tears.

I was so terrified to die, I prayed so hard that night,
'Please, don't let me die', I cried, I hoped the Preacher was right.

It took 15 years to answer that prayer, God heard every word,
I had to waste my life so bad, until His voice was heard.

Between 12 and salvation, I lived a life of sin,
I broke every moral law I'd known, destroying myself within.

When I finally met the Lord, I had nothing left inside,
He offered to exchange His life so blessed, for mine, of arrogance and pride.

I had pushed the moral barriers, way beyond their normal limits,
I never saw the pain I caused, I was far too caught up in it.

Looking at God from outside the Church, is hard to comprehend,
You are on the outside looking in, without a single friend.

But when you enter with an open heart, as humble as can be,
Jesus wraps His arms around you, forgives and sets you free.

So please don't think you are no good, He died to prove His love,
He wants you safely in His arms, to dwell in Heaven above.

No matter how sinful your life has been, There's none He won't forgive,
He puts the choosing in your hands, it's your choice where you live.

When people dress up really neat, they are honouring the Lord,
It doesn't mean they're above the rest, they just worship in one accord.

If you find that you're afraid to die, you can't see past the grave,
Come to Jesus, the Prince of Peace, You will never fear again.

No one is really good enough, we all are saved by grace,
But He's the only One I know, who died for the human race.

So if you want to live in peace, saturated in God's love,
Just think how blessed you truly are, to be called by God above.

He could have picked the High and mighty, or the King upon the throne,
The well-to-do business man, looking cool with his mobile phone.

But no, it is you God is calling, how privileged you must feel,
To believe with all your heart in something that you know to be real.

So, pick yourself up, keep running that race, don't stop until the end,
Your destiny is an eternity, with God, my privileged friend.

David T. Gilbert.

INTRODUCTION TO 'THE CHURCH'

THIS IS A poem I wrote to explain my views on how I see the Church, the many types of people who attend each week, and the main purposes and themes of why Church is so important. We all have our opinion and idea of the Church, but love it or hate it, Jesus laid His life down for the Church, establishing it for the purpose of being representative of His bride, and purifying it by His blood shed on the cross. His promise is to return very soon for His bride, for a complete, spotless, pure bride, so my advice to you is, get used to your family and let there be no divisions amongst you, because we are all one in Christ Jesus. May you be blessed as you read,

David T. Gilbert.

The Church

The Church is the place we meet with God,
On a regular weekly occasion,
Gathering to meet each Sunday on mass,
From every tribe and nation.

We meet in obedience to Christ's command,
To encourage and love one another,
Showing an attitude of mercy and grace,
To our Sister and our Brother.

Sunday is our family day with our kin,
A day to forgive and forget,
Making the most of opportunities we have,
To love without regret.

The Church is to house the vision of Christ,
To know where we are going,
The Spirit directs our every step,
Without Him, there's no knowing.

The Church is the place where miracles occur,
Of healing, salvation, and faith,
Where mercy, love and forgiveness reside,
Fitting for a spiritual place.

It's also the 'storehouse', where we bring our Tithe,
Which is holy to the Lord,
We give through faith and love for Him,
According to God's Word.

We all have unique talents and gifts,
Not everyone is the same,
But most of all, we are one in Christ,
In Him, there is no shame.

There are those who don't see eye to eye,
They openly disagree,
It's quite a challenge, to show God's love,
When some folk will not see.

If we fail to get things right down here,
We may never finish our race,
And miss our only chance in life,
To enter, by God's grace.

We need to practice Holiness,
Obeying God's every Word,
Thinking purely and doing good,
United in one accord.

When someone turns back to their sin,
A kind rebuke is required,
We help each other overcome,
Showing courage, as God desires.

Temptation is always challenging us,
We dare not yield or give in,
That's why we are one in Christ,
We make our stand for Him.

So if you say Church isn't for you,
Not quite your cup of tea,
It was Jesus who established the Church, my friend,
So that the blind may see.

The family of God is everywhere,
From every tribe and nation,
When Jesus comes back for His bride,
There will be much jubilation.

ACKNOWLEDGEMENTS AND DEDICATION

THIS IS BOTH an acknowledgement and a dedication to the one woman who has not only played a major part in the publishing of my books, but has spent the past 32 years trying to make me realise just how fortunate my life has been. Without her assistance and patient support, my books would never have been written, and I would have sadly missed my opportunity to be able to encourage the people that I have with my work. I refer to my wife, BessieMae, who I am still in love with to this day, and will still be in love with her till I pass away. BessieMae has been very important to me, especially with designing the front and back pages of books 2 &3, she has done really well.

I would also like to show my appreciation to my children, Donna, Joe and Daniel, who have been extremely supportive of my poetry, and have had to tolerate quite a bit at times.

Also, all of my friends at my local Church, who have believed in me enough to show their support for my venture. Some of them have lovingly, and honestly, scrutinised my work, giving me tips and suggestions on how I may improve my Poetry, making it more appealing and challenging to all who read my work.

But last, if not least, I thank my Lord for granting me the honour and privilege of drawing readers to my books, so that I am able to encourage as many as possible to a right attitude before God, and maybe include a few salvations along the way.

I honestly believe that I have managed to do what I was asked to do by God's Holy Spirit, and that is to publish my life story in two parts, before His return, even going as far as publishing a third book, just to show that it matters not who you are, but who you are believing in. To me, it is all about obedience and trust, obedience to God's humble voice, and trust in who He is, and what He is able to do with a humble, submissive heart.

In summary, I say THANK YOU to the God of all possibilities, for such a fortunate and blessed life, I would not exchange this life with God for all the pleasures this world has to offer. I leave you with one of my favourite scriptures, which has proven countless times to be total truth, Proverbs 3: 5 & 6. I pray that through my books, you may be inspired to find a deeper trust and unshakeable commitment in the one who loves you more than anyone else ever could,

David T. Gilbert.